This book belongs to:

_____

(Fill in your name!)

DATE STARTED: _____

Editor: Karrie Witkin
Art Director: Diane Shaw
Production Manager: Rebecca Westall

ISBN: 978-1-4197-4136-4

Printed and bound in China
10 9 8 7 6 5 4 3 2 1

Abrams Noterie products are available at special
discounts when purchased in quantity for premiums and
promotions as well as fundraising or educational use.
Special editions can also be created to specification.
For details, contact specialsales@abramsbooks.com
or the address below.

Abrams Noterie® is a registered
trademark of Harry N. Abrams, Inc.

ABRAMS The Art of Books
195 Broadway, New York, NY 10007
abramsbooks.com

MIX
Paper from
responsible sources
FSC™ C144853

You, Me, We!

BY ERIN JANG
(and Miles!)
Abrams Noterie
New York

A note from Erin...

Dear fellow parents ,

I created these activities with my 7-year-old son, Miles .

We were a dynamic team! My role in the project

was writing, designing & illustrating , and

Miles 's job was brainstorming activities & making

sure stuff was fun . In the process, we found out

more about each other! For example, I discovered that

gum-filled lollipops are his favorite candy,

and his superhero name would be CARTOON

NINJA Boy ! And I learned what makes

my son feel scared, stressed, and especially

loved (playing legos together & special gifts)!

I hope that you enjoy filling in these books with your

child as much as we loved making them!

...and Miles!

Dear fellow **kids** ,

I created these activities with **my mom** .

We were a **PERFECT** team! My role in the project

was **thinking of cool activities** , and

my mom. 's job was **doing everything**

else (haha) 😛 . In the process, we found out

more about each other! For example, I discovered that

-SOUR gummies are **her** favorite candy,

and **her** superhero name would be **⚡ ICED**

COFFEE GIRL ⚡ ! And I learned what makes

my mom feel scared, stressed, and especially

loved (**hug attacks and homemade cards**)!

I hope that you enjoy filling in these books with your

parent as much as we loved making them!

Portrait of Me

1. Switch books!
2. Sit across from your partner. Observe the specific things that make their face special.
3. Draw your partner's face in the frame, including all the important details.
4. Don't forget to sign your name below your art!

STUDY YOUR PARTNER'S:

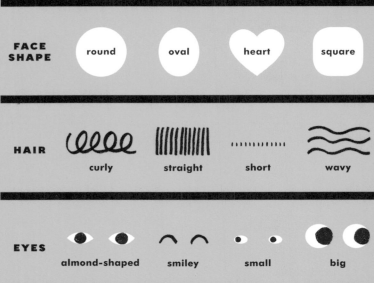

FACE SHAPE   round   oval   heart   square

HAIR   curly   straight   short   wavy

EYES   almond-shaped   smiley   small   big

DRAWN BY: _____

THIS OR THAT?

Which of the two choices do you like better? Check off the one you most prefer!

☐ Early bird
OR
☐ NIGHT OWL

☐ SWEET TREAT
OR
☐ SALTY SNACK

☐ Travel back in time!
OR
☐ Travel to the future!

☐ SPRING
OR
☐ Autumn

☐ Pancakes
OR
☐ WAFFLES

☐ **ADVENTURE**

OR

☐
Relaxation

☐ Outdoors!

OR

☐
Indoors!

☐ *Chocolate*

OR

☐
GUMMIES

☐ **MOUNTAIN** **OR** ☐ **OCEAN**

☐ **PIZZA**

OR

☐
Sushi

☐ **SOUP**

OR

☐ **SALAD**

☐
ROLLER COASTER

OR

☐
FERRIS WHEEL

☐ Ice cream

OR

☐
Popsicles

☐ **MUSIC**

OR

☐ **BOOKS**

☐ *Dress up* **OR** ☐ **Dress comfy**

I Love Treats!

What are your favorite special snacks?
Draw them in the spaces below.

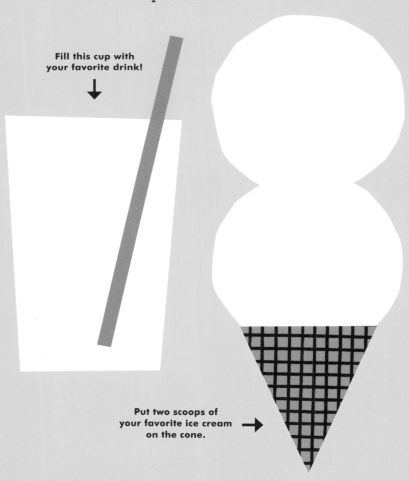

**Fill this cup with
your favorite drink!**

**Put two scoops of
your favorite ice cream
on the cone.**

What type of
snack should be
in this bag? Chips,
popcorn, pretzels,
or cookies?

→

Add your
favorite candy
to this jar!

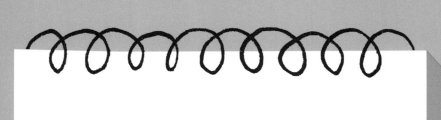

Write Me a Poem!

Q:
Where do poems come from?

1. Switch books!
2. Write the letters of the other person's name* vertically down the opposite page, in big letters.
3. Now use the letters on each line to write a word, phrase, or sentence to describe the other person. You're making an acrostic poem!
4. When you're done, exchange books and read the poem written for you.

Can't think of a word that starts with a certain letter? Turn the page to find fun suggestions, A to Z, that might inspire a phrase for your poem!

→

*KIDS: You can write Mom or Dad instead of your parent's first name!

A: Poe-trees!

Here are some words to help brainstorm ideas for your acrostic poem!

A

a
always
amazing
awesome
adventurous
admirable

does
dazzling
daring
dear
definitely
dynamic

D

G

goes
great
glad
genuine
gem
growing

H

happy
helpful
hug
heart
hooray
honestly

kind
kudos
kid
keen
knowledgeable
keeps

K

like
lovely
lively
learning
legendary
laughing

L

O

open
original
outstanding
out of this world
official
one

P

prefers
positively
plays
precious
pretty
phenomenal

so
super
special
silly
smart
strong

S

the
top
talented
totally
together
terrific

T

W

we
wow
wonderful
warm
winner
whiz

X

(e)xtra
(e)xtraordinar
(e)xcellent
(e)xtremely

B

best
bright
bighearted
biggest
brave
beautiful

C

cool
crazy
can
chief
creative
cheerful

extra
every
expert
excellent
eats
enjoys

E

fun
fan
favorite
fantastic
fond of
friend

F

I

is
incredible
interesting
intense
inspiring
indeed

J

just
joyful
jolly
jokester
jazzy
jubilant

my
most
master of
magical
magnificent
marvelous

M

neat
nice
number one
notably
never
naturally

N

Q

quick
quiet
quirky
quality
quintessential
queen

R

rad
really
remarkable
reliably
rock 'n' roll
radical

ultra
ultimate
über
unbelievably
unique
understanding

U

very
valuable
vibrant
vivid
vast
valiant

V

Y

yes
you
your
young
yeah
yowza

Z

zany
zealous
zest
zero
zippy

Crack the Code!

1. Switch books!
2. Using the alphabet key of symbols below, write a secret message for the other person to decode. Draw a picture for each letter in your note.
3. Swap books again. You and your partner can decode the messages written for each other!

Write a secret message here:

Decode the message here:

Invent a Code!

Now come up with your own secret code! Draw a symbol for each letter of the alphabet in the chart below, making sure each one is unique. Then make secret messages for each other using your codes.

Draw your secret alphabet!

A	B	C	D	E	F
G	H	I	J	K	L
M	N	O	P	Q	R
S	T	U	V	W	X
	Y	Z			

Write a secret message here:

Decode the message here:

Hand in Hand

1. Center your hand on the opposite page. Trace it carefully with a pencil.
2. Switch books!
3. In your partner's book, place your hand on top of their hand outline. Trace your hand again.
4. Switch books again! You should have your own book now, with two hand outlines.
5. Color in the spaces created by the overlapping outlines with different, contrasting colors.
6. Voilà! You now have your own piece of personal artwork.

PARENTS!
Make this project more interesting by outlining the hands of everyone in your family on a larger piece of paper!

Gifts!

What's one of the best gifts that you've received?

Why is it so special to you?

List three people you love.

1.

2.

3.

If money were no object, what would you give to each person above?

1.

2.

3.

Me & Hue

Answer the phrases below by drawing
a line from each one to a color on the page!

●
THE COLOR I WOULD BE IF I WERE A CRAYON

●
The color that reminds me of a fun memory

●
THE COLOR THAT MAKES ME FEEL SAD

●
The color that makes me feel happy

●
THE COLOR I THINK IS SUPER UGLY

PARENTS!
Ask your child why a certain color makes them happy or sad. Exchange stories about your fun color memory!

The color I would paint my room

THE COLOR I LOVE WEARING

The color of my favorite candy

Five Reasons

Switch books! Write down five (different and specific) things you love about the other person.

1

_____

_____

_____

_____

_____

_____

2

_____

_____

_____

_____

_____

3 _____

4 _____

5 _____

Fears!

Write down some things that you are afraid of.

Q: What are pirates afraid of?

*"I'm not afraid of storms,
for I'm learning how to
sail my own ship."*
Louisa May Alcott

Million-Dollar Questions

Q: When does it rain money?

ONE MILL

$

If you were given

$1,000,000

to spend on yourself right now,
what would you buy?

_____

_____

$

ONE MILL

DOLLARS

$

If you could give away

$1,000,000

to a good cause, which groups
or charities would you help?

_____

_____

$

DOLLARS

Silly Fill-in!

1. Switch books!
2. Fill in the blanks below with the first words that come to mind. When you're done, swap books again.
3. Now write the words from this page in the corresponding numbered spaces on the next page.
4. Read aloud your silly fill-in stories to each other!

1) Adjective	**5)** Number
2) Silly noun	**6)** Name of food
3) Silly noun above (plural)	**7)** Any flavor
4) Crazy type of transportation	**8)** Noun (plural)

9) Animal (plural)

15) Adjective

10) Imaginary creature (plural)

16) Color

11) Verb (past tense)

17) Type of hat (plural)

12) Excited sound

18) Any liquid

13) Food you've never tried

19) Favorite snack

14) Ordinary object

20) Happy saying

Our Silly Story!

One day, you and I took a(n) _____ (1)
trip to _____ (2) City,
which is famous for its _____ (3).
We woke up early and traveled to the city by
_____ (4). It took us _____ (5)
hours to get there! Once we arrived, we were
so hungry. We went to a cool café that served
_____ (6) toast and
_____ (7) juice.
Then we went to see an incredible show that
featured singing _____ (8),
dancing _____ (9),
fire-breathing _____ (10),
and acrobats that _____ (11)
through the air! I just couldn't stop exclaiming,
"_____ (12)!"
After the show, we walked around the city,

tried some _____ (13)
ice cream, and got tickets to visit the amazing

_____ (14)
museum. We really learned so much from that

_____ (15) experience!
For dinner, we went to a restaurant where the

waiters wore fancy _____ (16)
suits and the guests wore their most fabulous

_____ (17).
Everyone sipped fizzy _____ (18)
in crystal glasses with their pinkies up, and our

dinner was served on impossibly tiny dishes. We

were still hungry after this meal, so we stopped

by a street cart selling hot dogs, pretzels, and

_____ (19). We bought
one of each and then sat on the sidewalk to eat.

"_____ (20),"

we both said. It was the perfect end to a super

memorable trip.

Tree of Gratitude

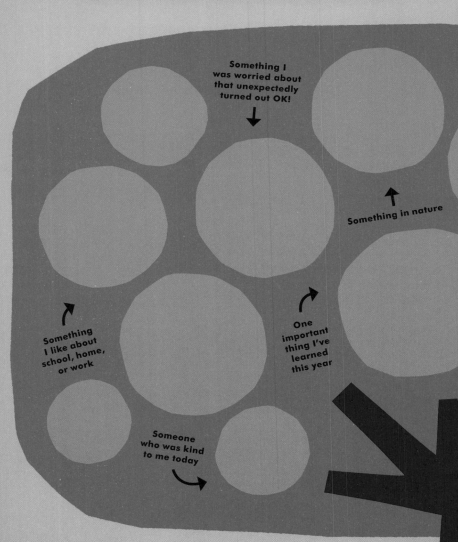

Something I was worried about that unexpectedly turned out OK!

Something in nature

Something I like about school, home, or work

One important thing I've learned this year

Someone who was kind to me today

Find a quiet spot. Take time to think about all the good things in your life, big and small. Write down really specific things you're thankful for below. Respond to the prompts inside the tree to jumpstart your gratitude!

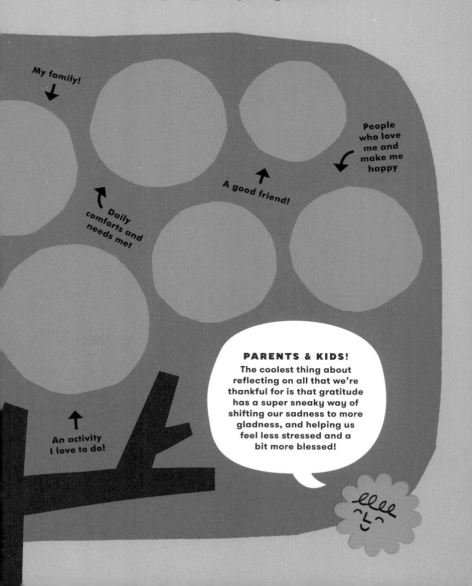

My family!

People who love me and make me happy

A good friend!

Daily comforts and needs met

An activity I love to do!

PARENTS & KIDS!
The coolest thing about reflecting on all that we're thankful for is that gratitude has a super sneaky way of shifting our sadness to more gladness, and helping us feel less stressed and a bit more blessed!

Super-Me!

Draw yourself as a superhero with a cool costume and unique superpowers!

SUPERHERO NAME

MY SUPERPOWERS

EVIL FORCES TO CONQUER

Ode to Joy

What are the things that bring you joy? List ten things (big and small) that make you feel super happy.

2.

3.

1.

4.

6.

5.

PARENTS!
Encourage your child
to consider what brings
them joy on a deeper
level. For example, you
might want to ask your
child what fills up their
love tank? Or what are
some of the things that
make them happy that
cannot be bought?

7.

8.

10.

9.

May I Suggest...

Draw and write your favorite recommendations in the spaces below!

Think of a book you love that you would recommend to someone else. Write the title and draw on the empty book cover!

Write down a favorite song!

What TV show do you like to watch?

Which game do you like to play?

PARENTS!
Take this exercise a step further:

1. Have a family night where you watch an episode of your favorite childhood TV show and then one from your child's current favorite series.

2. Make playlists for each other!

3. Choose a book you loved when you were your kid's age, then ask them to choose a book. Take turns reading them together!

1. Switch books!
2. In your partner's book, make up a crazy tongue twister. Start with your partner's first name,* and then make a sentence by adding at least six to eight more words that start with the same letter (short connector words like "a" and "the" are allowed).
3. Swap books again. See who can say their tongue twister the fastest!

*KIDS: You can write Mom or Dad instead of your parent's first name!

Need an example?

HERE'S A CLASSIC: *She sells seashells by the seashore.*

AND ANOTHER: *Magical Miles makes a million magnetic mega monsters!*

TWISTER!

Away We Go!

**What's one favorite place
we've visited together as a family?**

What were your favorite things we did there?

List five other places you would like to visit someday!

1. _____

2. _____

3. _____

4. _____

5. _____

Check off the things you like doing best when traveling!

☐ exploring nature

☐ visiting museums

☐ trying new food

☐ shopping at fun markets

☐ watching movies on the plane

☐ visiting family or friends

☐ riding bikes

☐ walking everywhere

☐ looking at art

☐ playing outdoor sports

☐ seeing unique architecture

☐ using a different language

☐ _____

Best Day Ever!

If you could plan the most fantastic, super amazing, best day ever, what would your day look like? Who would you spend it with, where would you go and which activities would you plan? Be as specific as possible! Use your imagination to make your dream schedule.

7:00 AM

8:00 AM

9:00 AM

10:00 AM

11:00 AM

12:00 PM

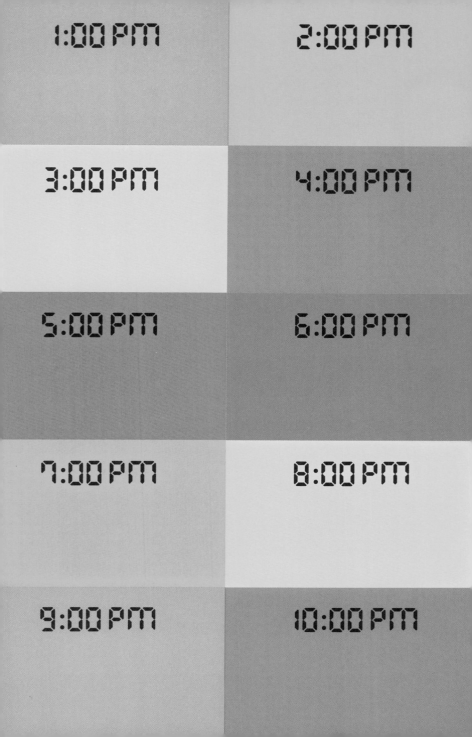

Dream

*What is dreamstorming, you ask?
It's a combination of brainstorming and
dreaming big! Don't get caught up about what
might feel unrealistic, risky, or impossible—
write down all the crazy ideas, big and small!*

DREAMSTORM HERE!

storming!

1. Dreamstorm about things you want to learn or try! You could include a new skill, a sport, a language, or something you don't feel confident doing.
2. Set a timer for five minutes and write down as many things as you can in the space to the left. When the time is up, underline a few things from your list that you really want to try in the coming year.
3. Share your dreamstorm with your partner and see if you have any in common!

TIP!
Choose one activity that you both wrote down and underlined and make a concrete plan to learn or try it together!

Me-moji!

What makes you feel your feelings? Try to remember the last time you felt these emotions and fill in the blanks beside each emoji.

I feel happy when

I feel sad when

I feel stressed when

I feel relaxed when

I feel frustrated when

I feel loved when

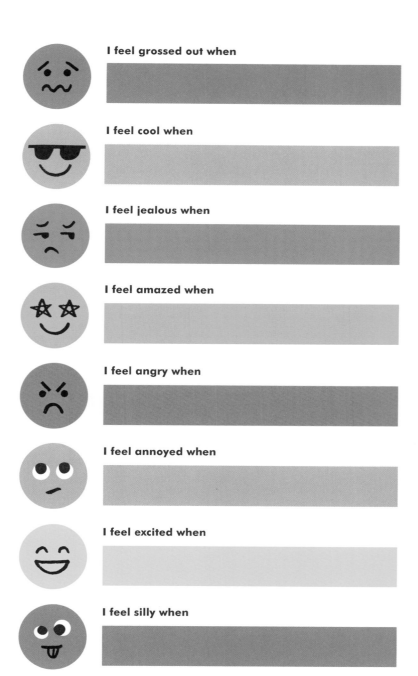

I feel grossed out when

I feel cool when

I feel jealous when

I feel amazed when

I feel angry when

I feel annoyed when

I feel excited when

I feel silly when

Museum
of Me

TIP!
Think about the things
that you love, objects
you treasure most,
things you worked on or
created that you're proud
of, important moments,
or anything else that
means a lot to you!

Imagine a museum is creating an exhibit all
about *you*. What important objects and artifacts
would be on display? Draw your treasured objects
on the pedestals and shelves, and fill the frames
with important moments in your life!

D.I.Y. Cootie Catcher!

1. Carefully cut out the square on the next page with scissors.
2. Write a different silly command on the lines in the eight inside triangles (see some examples below!).
3. Follow the step-by-step instructions on the next pages to create each fold until you are finished. Then, play!

SOME SILLY COMMANDS TO TRY!

Make a really funny face.

Give me the biggest hug!

Say a nice compliment!

Tell me a good joke!

Pat your head while rubbing your belly.

Two-minute back massage!

Try saying the alphabet backwards.

Ten jumping jacks as fast as you can.

TICKLE ATTACK!

Or anything ridiculous, funny, or nice you want the other person to do!

*Cut out the template above,
then follow the steps on the next page!*

FOLDING INSTRUCTIONS:

1. Place your sheet face down (yellow back side up). Fold and unfold two times.

2. Fold the corners into the center.

3. Flip over.

4. Fold corners into the center.

5. Flip over.

6. Fold in half.

7. Then, unfold.

8. Now fold in half the other way.

9. Then insert your fingers in the four pockets to play! *(See below.)*

HOW TO PLAY!

1. Ask your partner to pick one of the four colors. Then spell the word ("B-L-U-E") while opening and closing the cootie catcher for each letter.
2. Your partner then chooses one of the visible numbers in the open side. Open and close the cootie catcher each time as you count up to the chosen number. ("1-2-3-4-5...!")
3. Have your partner choose a number again. Lift the flap below the number and read the command that your partner must do!

Wild Thing!

Q: What do you call a bear with no teeth?

If I were an animal,* I would be a

because

Draw a picture of yourself as this animal!

KIDS!
Once you're done, choose an animal that best represents your mom or dad, and explain why! Then ask them to choose an animal that is most like you!

*Try thinking about what characteristics are unique to you, and which animal might have those same qualities to match! Are you funny like a monkey or fearless like a lion? Need extra inspiration? Turn the page!

→

A : A gummy bear!

Here are some personality traits we like to associate with animals!

BEAR
big
cuddly
lazy

CAT
clever
curious
independent

CHEETAH
fast runner
spontaneous
smart

DEER
shy
graceful
sensitive

ELEPHANT
strong
steadfast
trustworthy

GIRAFFE
tall
gentle
confident

HORSE
faithful
brave
noble

MOUSE
quiet
small
introvert

OCTOPUS
multitasker
creative
mysterious

OWL
wise
observant
stays up late

RHINOCEROS
tough
unstoppable
thick-skinned

SONGBIRD
lyrical
joyful
optimistic

TIGER
powerful
courageous
fierce

BEAVER
helpful
earnest
hardworking

BEES
busy
productive
team player

BUTTERFLY
lighthearted
beautiful
delightful

DOG
loyal
affectionate
enthusiastic

DOLPHIN
playful
happy
extroverted

EAGLE
leader
serious
focused

KOALA
cute
easygoing
gentle

LION
ambitious
fearless
proud

MONKEY
silly
mischievous
great climber

PARROT
talkative
colorful
comedic

PEACOCK
outgoing
fashionable
flamboyant

PENGUIN
formal
funny
cooperative

TURTLE
patient
steady
slow

WHALE
deep
thinker
soulful

ZEBRA
dynamic
unique
wild

Make Your Mascot

_____

_____

_____

_____ !

1. Choose your favorite animal or creature that best represents you. (Look at the previous page for inspiration!)
2. Choose two of your favorite colors.

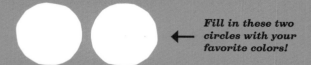

← _Fill in these two circles with your favorite colors!_

3. Pick something cool for your mascot to wear. (Special glasses or a hat?)
4. Draw your mascot in the space provided using your two favorite colors!
5. Come up with an encouraging cheer or chant for your mascot to say! Write it in the speech balloon.

My Crew

Who are the important people in your life?
Write your name in the center oval, then jot down
the names of the people close to you, starting with
your family. As you branch out, fill in the circles
with other relatives, friends, teachers, and people
you spend time with and who care about you. When
you're done, study your charts together.

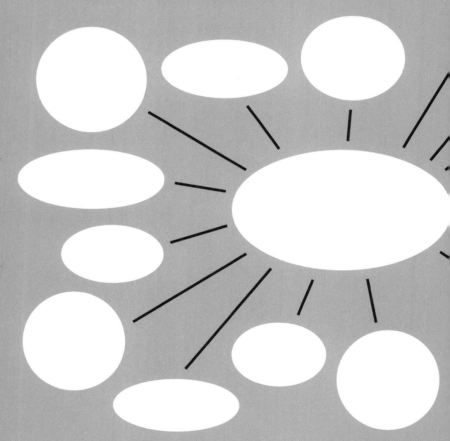

Imaginary Inventions

If you could invent one thing to make the world a better, kinder, and happier place for all, what would you create? To begin, brainstorm some ideas below:

THE WORLD NEEDS LESS:

AND COULD USE MORE:

I WISH FOR MORE

IN THE WORLD, FOR EVERYBODY.

Now, fire up your creativity engine! Using the ideas you wrote above, imagine an invention that could help make the world a better place for everyone. Sketch it in the space to the right, and give your invention a name.

MY INVENTION: _____

HEY, INVENTOR!
Could it be a kindness machine?
A magical garden that grows what
the world needs? A flying bicycle
supercharged by something special?
Dream up something original and
consider how you could multiply
good in the world!

My/Your Uniform

Add your skin color, hair, shoes, and favorite accessories.

Your uniform is your favorite outfit—what you would wear every day if you could! Draw and color yourself head to toe, wearing the clothes you feel your best in. Then imagine your partner's favorite outfit and draw it here!

Coupon-a-Day!

Here are seven coupons for each day of the week. Fill in the coupons with one kind act for every day. Then, carefully cut each coupon out with scissors. Staple the coupons together on the left side to make a special booklet. Give the mini coupon book to your partner to redeem at any time!

KIDS!

How can you make your parent's day a little brighter and easier? Maybe offer to do chores or finish homework early. Coupons for extra hugs and kisses are always a slam dunk.

PARENTS!

What fills up your kid's love tank the most? One-on-one time? Movie night (their choice)? A favorite candy in their lunchbox? Bonus screen time? (YUP.)

A COUPON BOOK FOR:

_____

MONDAY

THIS COUPON IS GOOD FOR:

_____

Never expires!

TUESDAY

THIS COUPON IS GOOD FOR:

_____

Never expires!

WEDNESDAY

THIS COUPON IS GOOD FOR:

_____

Never expires!

THURSDAY

THIS
COUPON
IS GOOD
FOR:

_____

Never expires!

FRIDAY

THIS
COUPON
IS GOOD
FOR:

_____

Never expires!

SATURDAY

THIS
COUPON
IS GOOD
FOR:

_____

Never expires!

SUNDAY

THIS
COUPON
IS GOOD
FOR:

_____

Never expires!